English
Rapid Tests 1

Siân Goodspeed

Schofield & Sims

Introduction

This book gives you practice in answering English questions quickly.

The questions are like the questions on the 11+ and other school selection tests. You must find the correct answers.

School selection tests are usually timed, so you need to get used to working quickly. Each test has a target time for you to work towards. Ask an adult to time you.

What you need

- A pencil
- An eraser
- A clock, watch or stopwatch
- An adult to time you and to mark the test for you

What to do

- Turn to **Section 1 Test 1** on page 4. Look at the grey box at the top of the page labelled **Target time**. This tells you how long the test should take.
- The adult helping you will tell you when to begin.
- Read each question carefully and then write the answer on the answer line. Sometimes you need to tick or underline the correct answer instead.
- Try to answer every question. If you do get stuck on a question, leave it and go on to the next one. Work quickly and try your best.
- Each test is two pages long. When you reach the end, stop and tell the adult that you have finished.
- The adult will mark your test. Then the adult will fill in the **Score**, **Time taken** and **Target met?** boxes at the end of the test.
- Turn to the **Progress chart** on page 40. Write your score in the box and colour in the graph to show how many questions you got right.
- Did you get some questions wrong? You should always have another go at them before you look at the answers. Then ask the adult to check your work and help you if you are still not sure.
- Later, you will do some more of these tests. You will soon learn to work through them more quickly. The adult who is helping you will tell you what to do next.

Published by **Schofield & Sims Ltd**,
7 Mariner Court, Wakefield, West Yorkshire WF4 3FL, UK
Telephone 01484 607080
www.schofieldandsims.co.uk

This edition copyright © Schofield & Sims Ltd, 2018
First published in 2018

Author: **Siân Goodspeed**. Siân Goodspeed has asserted her moral rights under the Copyright, Designs and Patents Act, 1988, to be identified as the author of this work. Any text not otherwise attributed has been written by Siân Goodspeed and is copyright © Schofield & Sims Ltd, 2018.

Five Little Chickens (page 10) is by Anonymous. **Penny Dreadful is Incredibly Contagious** (page 22) is an extract from Penny Dreadful is Incredibly Contagious by Joanna Nadin (Copyright © Joanna Nadin, 2013). Reprinted by permission of A.M. Heath & Co Ltd. **Wind on the Hill** (page 28) is an extract from Now We Are Six by A. A. Milne. Text copyright © The Trustees of the Pooh Properties 1927. Published by Egmont UK Ltd and used with permission. **My Naughty Little Sister Goes Fishing** (page 34) is an extract from My Naughty Little Sister Goes Fishing by Dorothy Edwards. Text copyright © 1976 Dorothy Edwards. Published by Egmont UK Ltd and used with permission.

Every effort has been made to trace all copyright holders and obtain their permission to reproduce copyright material prior to publication. If notified, the publisher will rectify any errors or omissions at the earliest opportunity.

British Library Cataloguing in Publication Data. A catalogue record for this book is available from the British Library.

Design by **Ledgard Jepson Ltd**
Front cover design by **Ledgard Jepson Ltd**
Printed in the UK by **Page Bros (Norwich) Ltd**

ISBN 978 07217 1429 5

Contents

A **pull-out answers section** (pages A1 to A12) appears in the centre of this book, between pages 20 and 21. It also gives simple guidance on how best to use this book. Remove this section before the child begins working through the tests.

Target time: **12 minutes**

Read the text and answer the questions below.

A Letter

Dear Harry,

How are you? Are you having a good summer? Mum tells me you are going on holiday to France soon. I hope you have a great time.

5 We have just come back from our family holiday in Spain. We had a fantastic trip! The weather was really sunny and hot. We spent most days at the seaside, building sandcastles and swimming in the sea. I also had a go at water-skiing. The first time, I found it really tricky, but the second time I started to get the hang of it. It was really thrilling, zipping along behind the boat with the sea spraying in my face.

We stayed in a huge villa with a pretty garden and a private pool. I shared a room with Tom, which
10 we haven't done since we lived in Spring Cottage, and he was only a baby then. It was quite fun, as we stayed up late chatting and reading most nights, but sometimes Tom's snoring kept me awake!

It was so hot on the first day that I got sunburnt, even though I was wearing sun cream and a sun hat. My nose was the most burnt – it went bright red. Mum said I looked
15 like Rudolf the Reindeer! We had a wonderful holiday but it is nice to be back home in England, because the weather is a bit cooler and I can sleep in my own bedroom.

Anyway, got to go! See you soon!

20 From your best friend,

Jake ☺

Write **A**, **B**, **C** or **D** on the answer line.

1. Who is the letter from?

   A Harry

   B Jake

   C Thomas

   D Mum

   _____   /1

2. What is the relationship between Harry and Jake?

   A They are brothers.

   B They are cousins.

   C They are friends.

   D They are neighbours.

   _____   /1

3. Where has Jake been on holiday?

   A Spain

   B France

   C England

   D He has not been on holiday yet.

   _____   /1

4. Which water sport did Jake learn to do on holiday?

   A surfing

   B scuba-diving

   C snorkelling

   D water-skiing

   _____   /1

5. What <u>two</u> activities did Jake spend most of his holiday doing?

_____ and _____   /2

6. Which <u>two</u> words match what Jake thinks about water-skiing? Tick the boxes.

difficult ☐   slow ☐   easy ☐   exciting ☐   stupid ☐   /2

7. What kept Jake awake on some nights?

_____

_____   /2

8. What happened to Jake's nose?

_____

_____   /2

9. Give <u>two</u> reasons why Jake was happy to be back at home.

_____

_____

_____

_____   /4

10. Read the passage below. Choose the word in **bold** that best fits in the sentence and underline it.

Whenever I go to the seaside, I take my bucket and spade so that I can **a) build / carry / lose**

sandcastles. Sometimes, if I am feeling **b) afraid / scared / creative**, I make something a

bit different. One year, I made a huge sand dragon with enormous **c) wings / fur / neck** and

a long, scaly tail. I even made sand flames coming out of its **d) breathing / nostrils / fire**!

I am always very proud of my sand **e) spades / sculptures / beaches**, so I do feel a bit sad

when the **f) tide / wind / rock** comes in and washes them away.   /6

Score:		Time taken:		Target met?	

Target time: **12 minutes**

1. Read the sentences below. Underline the correct verb form in each set of brackets.

    Example: I always (<u>jump</u> jumped jumping) high on my trampoline.

    a) Yesterday, Rena (walk   walking   walked) to school.

    b) On Mondays, my sister (sings   singing   sang) in a choir.

    c) Today, I (eat   ate   eaten) three bananas!

    d) Susie (was   were   is) proud when she won the medal.

    /4

2. Choose the best word, **and** or **but**, to complete each sentence. Write it on the line.

    Example: I like coffee <u> but </u> I don't like tea.

    a) I have a pet dog _____ a pet cat.

    b) My sister can drive _____ she hasn't taken her test yet.

    c) Our teacher likes milk _____ sugar in her tea.

    d) It was cold outside _____ Ellie refused to wear her coat.

    /4

3. In each of the sentences below, <u>two</u> of the words have swapped places. Work out which words need to be swapped for the sentence to make sense. Underline the two words.

    Example: My <u>likes</u> <u>sister</u> playing football.

    a) The film very was funny.

    b) I holiday going on am.

    c) Jax ate dinner for pizza.

    d) Natalie enjoyed the party birthday.

    /4

Schofield & Sims

4. The sentences below are missing their punctuation. Write out each sentence on the line, adding in the correct sentence punctuation.

Example: my brother likes cheese   <u>My brother likes cheese.</u>

a) where are you going

_____

b) stop right there

_____

c) which colour do you like best

_____

d) giraffes are my favourite animals

_____

/4

5. The passage below has had some words removed. Choose the correct words from the box. Write the missing words on the lines. You may use each word only once.

finding	kept	picks
picked	watching	collected
watches	puts	digs
let	digging	putting

My little sister likes **a)** _____ up worms in the garden. When she finds

one, she **b)** _____ it up by one end and **c)** _____ it

wriggle about. Then she **d)** _____ it into her wormery. One day, my

sister **e)** _____ 36 worms. They didn't all fit in her wormery, so she

f) _____ most of them go.

/6

| Score: | | Time taken: | | Target met? | |

Target time: **12 minutes**

1. Draw lines to match the words to their contractions.

    she will   they're

    they are   what's

    what is   we've

    we have   she'll

    /4

2. Add the suffix **–ness** or **–ment** to each of the words below to change them into nouns. Write the new word on the line.

    Example: shy   _shyness_

    a) punish   _____

    b) bright   _____

    c) happy   _____

    d) amaze   _____

    /4

3. Decide which of the words in bold is the correct word for each sentence. Underline the word.

    Example: Maddy was wearing a **plain** / **plane** scarf.

    a) Lorenzo tried to **pour** / **poor** the juice into the glass.

    b) It would **seem** / **seam** that we are lost!

    c) You need **flour** / **flower** to make bread.

    d) I ate a **hole** / **whole** chicken for dinner.

    /4

4. Each sentence below contains an incomplete word. Write out the sentence on the line, filling in the missing letters to spell the word correctly.

Example: I **wo** ___ ___ **d** like to see the ballet.   <u>I would like to see the ballet.</u>

a) There are 30 **childr** ___ ___ in my class.

_____

b) Sophie bought some new **clot** ___ ___ **s** in the sale.

_____

c) I think my mother is really **be** ___ ___ **tiful**.

_____

d) Malek fell **beh** ___ ___ **d** with his piano practice.

_____

/4

5. Underline the word in each set of brackets that means the <u>opposite</u> of the word in bold.

Example: up   (left   yes   <u>down</u>)

a) **light**   (bright   heavy   star)

b) **quick**   (slick   fast   slow)

c) **weak**   (day   strong   sick)

d) **dodge**   (avoid   hard   meet)

e) **soft**   (fluffy   wet   hard)

f) **near**   (far   here   long)

/6

Score:		Time taken:		Target met?	

Target time: **12 minutes**

Read the text and answer the questions below.

Five Little Chickens, by Anonymous

Said the first little chicken,
With a queer little squirm,
"Oh, I wish I could find
A fat little worm!"

5   Said the next little chicken,
With an odd little shrug,
"Oh, I wish I could find
A fat little bug!"

Said the third little chicken,
10 With a sharp little squeal,
"Oh, I wish I could find
Some nice yellow meal!"

Said the fourth little chicken,
With a small sigh of grief,
15 "Oh, I wish I could find
A green little leaf!"

Said the fifth little chicken,
With a faint little moan,
"Oh, I wish I could find
20 A wee gravel-stone!"

"Now, see here," said the mother,
From the green garden-patch,
"If you want any breakfast,
You must come and scratch."

Write **A**, **B**, **C** or **D** on the answer line.

1. What type of text is this?

A a story

B a poem

C instructions

D a report

_____ /1

2. What are all the little chickens complaining about?

A They are bored.

B They are hungry.

C They are lost.

D They are tired.

_____ /1

3. Which word in the text means 'wriggle'?

A shriek

B hoot

C squirm

D jump

_____ /1

4. Which word in the text means 'groan'?

A moan

B grief

C shrug

D faint

_____ /1

5. What does the first little chicken wish for?

_____   /2

6. What action does the second little chicken do?

_____   /2

7. Which <u>two</u> colour words are found in the text? Tick the boxes.

yellow ☐   red ☐   green ☐   brown ☐   black ☐   /2

8. What does the fourth little chicken want to find?

_____   /2

9. **a)** What does the chickens' mother say they should do?

_____   /2

b) Look at the words in the box below. Tick the <u>two</u> words that you think best describe the chickens' mother when she says this.

scared ☐   lonely ☐   brisk ☐   caring ☐   embarrassed ☐   /2

10. Draw lines to match the rhyming words in the poem.

grief   bug

patch   stone

moan   worm

squeal   leaf

shrug   scratch

squirm   meal   /6

| Score: | | Time taken: | | Target met? | |

Target time: **12 minutes**

1. Change each word in bold into an adverb so that the sentence makes sense. Write the adverb on the line.

   Example: Emma ran **quick** down the road.   _quickly_

   a) I ate my dinner **slow**.   _____

   b) My sister **kind** gave me her last sweet.   _____

   c) Leona danced **happy** to her music.   _____

   d) Oliver's dad shouted **angry**.   _____

   /4

2. Choose the best word, **because** or **if**, to complete each sentence. Write it on the line.

   Example: I walk to school _if_ the weather is good.

   a) I ride my bike to school _____ it keeps me fit.

   b) Amelia's cousin will buy a car _____ she passes her driving test.

   c) I am allowed to stay up late tonight _____ it's the school holidays.

   d) She might lose her pencil case _____ she doesn't put her name in it.

   /4

3. Each sentence below is missing a punctuation mark. Add in the missing full stop, question mark or exclamation mark at the end of each sentence.

   Example: Do you like grapes _?_

   a) How old are you _____

   b) That's not fair _____

   c) I hate cheese _____

   d) My name is Sara _____

   /4

4. Write out each sentence on the line, changing it from the present to the past tense.

Example: I walk to the park.　　　I walked to the park.

a) Jamie swims fast.

_____

b) My mum drinks a cup of tea.

_____

c) Elodie climbs the tree.

_____

d) I leap over the fence.

_____

/4

5. The passage below has had some words removed. Choose the correct words from the box. Write the missing words on the lines. You may use each word only once.

purr	nose	lap
lively	tip	kitten
lazy	claws	ears
teeth	pet	paws

I have two **a)** _____ cats called Smudge and Fluffy. They are quite

b) _____ cats – all they do is eat and sleep. Smudge has black fur

apart from his four white **c)** _____. Fluffy is all white apart from the

d) _____ of his tail. They love to sit on my **e)** _____

and they always **f)** _____ loudly when I stroke them.

/6

Score:		Time taken:		Target met?	

Target time: **12 minutes**

1. Each sentence below contains an incomplete word. Write out the sentence on the line, filling in the missing letters to spell the word correctly.

    Example: I **wo** __ __ **d** like to see the ballet.   *I would like to see the ballet.*

    a) I like to **padd** __ __ in the paddling pool.

    _____

    b) It was a truly **magic** __ __ show.

    _____

    c) There are 20 **peop** __ __ on the bus.

    _____

    d) Sheena won a **speci** __ __ award for her hard work.

    _____

    /4

2. Write out the words in each row on the line so that they are in alphabetical order.

    Example: hope brick wand swap   *brick hope swap wand*

    a) drive bank circle fair

    _____

    b) lion tiger mice olive

    _____

    c) wand vine trick under

    _____

    d) sheep plant right quick

    _____

    /4

3. Decide which of the words in bold is the correct word for each sentence. Underline the word.

Example: Maddy was wearing a **plain** / **plane** scarf.

a) Can you **see** / **sea** all the sailing boats?

b) Of **course** / **coarse** you can sit next to me!

c) I will **right** / **write** her a letter.

d) Which is the best **root** / **route** to the park?

/4

4. Add the suffix **–ful** or **–less** to each of the words below to change them into adjectives. Write the new word on the line.

Example: play   _playful_

a) wire   _____

b) hate .   _____

c) boast   _____

d) home   _____

/4

5. Underline the word in each set of brackets that is <u>closest</u> in meaning to the word in bold.

Example: big   (small   run   <u>large</u>)

a) **centre**   (edge   round   middle)

b) **squash**   (sit   crush   open)

c) **intelligent**   (dull   clever   happy)

d) **cancel**   (stop   start   count)

e) **damage**   (break   fix   danger)

f) **chuckle**   (cry   shout   giggle)

/6

Score:		Time taken:		Target met?	

Read the text and answer the questions below.

FUN WITH FLOWERS

Daisy chains

Daisy chains are a perfect outdoor activity for a sunny day. They are quick and easy to make, and you can use them to create gorgeous crowns, necklaces and bracelets for you and your friends. To make your own, follow the instructions below.

5 1. Pick a daisy. For best results, choose daisies with long, wide stems.

2. Using your thumbnail, make a slit near the bottom of the stem, taking care not to split it in half.

3. Pick another daisy and thread its stem through the slit of the first daisy.

4. Pull the stem gently through until the flower is up against the slit.

10 5. Keep repeating this process until you are happy with the length of your daisy chain.

6. Finish your chain by making a second slit in the first daisy and threading the last daisy through to create a loop.

Pressing flowers

Pressed flowers make great decorations. They are also brilliant for using in art projects such as birthday cards. Simply place a few fresh flowers in between two sheets of card and then put the whole thing in the middle of a heavy book. Leave inside the book for about two weeks before carefully removing the pressed flowers.

Write **A**, **B**, **C** or **D** on the answer line.

1. What type of text is this?

A a story

B a poem

C instructions

D a report

_____ /1

2. What kind of day is perfect for making daisy chains?

A a windy day

B a sunny day

C a cold day

D a boring day

_____ /1

3. What should you use to slit the daisy stem?

A a knife

B scissors

C your thumbnail

D your teeth

_____ /1

4. What should you take care not to do when you make a slit in the stem?

A pull off the leaves

B cut yourself

C squash the flower

D split the stem in half

_____ /1

5. Name <u>two</u> types of jewellery you can make with daisy chains.

_____ and _____   /2

6. What should you do with the stem of the second daisy?

_____

_____   /2

7. In line 10, what does 'Keep repeating this process' mean?

_____

_____   /2

8. What can pressed flowers be used for?

_____

_____   /2

9. Which of the two flower activities would be best if you only had one afternoon?
Explain your answer.

_____

_____

_____

_____   /4

10. Read the passage below. Choose the word in bold that best fits in the sentence and underline it.

Daisies **a) are / involve / belong** to one of the largest plant families in the world.

They are found everywhere on Earth **b) also / except / include** Antarctica. There are

many different **c) types / flower / plant** of daisy. The common daisy, with its white

d) stem / petals / leaf and yellow centre, is the one you are most likely to

e) find / fix / sit in your **f) pond / tree / garden**.   /6

Score:		Time taken:		Target met?	

Target time: **12 minutes**

1. Read the sentences below and look at the words in bold. Change the past tense into the present tense by changing the words in bold. Write the new words on the line.

   The first one has been done for you.

Past tense	Present tense
Example: I **was jumping** on my trampoline.	_am jumping_
a) I **was singing** in the bath.	_____
b) Elena **was eating** an apple.	_____
c) You **were telling** a story.	_____
d) We **were riding** our bikes.	_____

/4

2. The sentences below are missing their capital letters. Write out each sentence on the line, adding in the correct capital letters. There may be more than one missing from each sentence.

   Example: we like eating bananas.　　_We like eating bananas._

   a) our dog spot has a long tail.

   _____

   b) do i look older than you?

   _____

   c) her sister is called milly.

   _____

   d) the flowers look very pretty.

   _____

   e) we went to the cinema on saturday.

   _____

   f) she asked me if i liked her.

   _____

/6

3. Underline the noun in each sentence.

   Example: I have a very big <u>bed</u>.

   a) Our caravan is bright red.

   b) He enjoys listening to loud music.

   c) I dropped my dinner when I tripped up.

   d) She loves opening presents!

/4

4. In each of the sentences below, <u>two</u> of the words have swapped places. Work out which words need to be swapped for the sentence to make sense. Underline the two words.

   Example: My <u>likes</u> <u>sister</u> playing football.

   a) How is old your cat?

   b) His Jackson is name.

   c) I school to walk.

   d) chocolate like I biscuits.

/4

5. Read the sentences below. Underline the correct verb form in each set of brackets.

   Example: I always (<u>jump</u>   jumped   jumping) high on my trampoline.

   a) Yesterday, I (run   running   ran) to catch the bus.

   b) Each Saturday, my mum (gives   gave   giving) me some pocket money.

   c) Last week, Sammy (gone   goes   went) to the zoo.

   d) Alicia (done   do   did) well in her running race.

/4

Score:		Time taken:		Target met?	

Target time: **12 minutes**

1. Write the plural form of each word on the line.

Example: house ___houses___

a) turkey _____

b) factory _____

c) goat _____

d) trolley _____

/4

2. One word in each set does not go with the others. Underline this odd word out.

Example: paint draw scribble <u>dance</u>

a) run skip sleep hop

b) giggle smile sob laugh

c) cold hot warm boiling

d) red blue whale pink

/4

3. In each sentence below, there is an incorrectly spelt word. Find the word, underline it and then write the correct spelling on the line.

Example: She found the test <u>dificult</u>. ___difficult___

a) On suny days, Noah loves to play outside in his garden. _____

b) You should allways wash your hands before dinner. _____

c) She loves skiping races with her friend. _____

d) I enjoy dancing so much that I never feel like stoping! _____

/4

Notes for parents, tutors, teachers and other adult helpers

- **English Rapid Tests 1** is designed for six- and seven-year-olds, but may also be suitable for some older children.

- Remove this pull-out section before giving the book to the child.

- Before the child begins work on the first test, together read the instructions headed **What to do** on page 2. As you do so, point out to the child the suggested **Target time** for completing the test.

- Make sure the child has all the equipment in the list headed **What you need** on page 2.

- There are three sections in this book. Each section contains two comprehension tests, two grammar and punctuation tests, and two spelling and vocabulary tests.

- Be sure that the child knows to tell you clearly when he or she has finished the test.

- When the child is ready, say 'Start the test now' and make a note of the start time.

- When the child has finished, make a note of the end time and then work out how long he or she took to complete the test. Then fill in the **Time taken** box, which appears at the end of the test.

- Mark the child's work using this pull-out section. Each test is out of 22 marks and each correct answer is worth one mark unless otherwise stated in the answers. Then complete the **Score** box at the end of the test.

- For all spelling questions, the answer must be spelt correctly for the full mark to be awarded. In the comprehension tests, the child does not need to write in full sentences for the marks to be awarded.

- This table shows you how to mark the **Target met?** box and the **Action** notes help you to plan the next step. However, these are suggestions only. Please use your own judgement as you decide how best to proceed.

Score	Time taken	Target met?	Action
$1-11\frac{1}{2}$	Any	Not yet	Provide help and support as needed.
$12-17\frac{1}{2}$	Any	Not yet	Encourage the child to keep practising using the tests in this book. The child may need to repeat some tests. If so, wait a few weeks or the child may simply remember the correct answers. Provide help and support as needed.
18–22	Over target – child took too long	Not yet	
18–22	On target – child took suggested time or less	Yes	Encourage the child to keep practising using further tests in this book, and to move on to the next book when you think this is appropriate.

- After finishing each test, the child should fill in the **Progress chart** on page 40.

- Whatever the test score, always encourage the child to have another go at the questions that he or she got wrong – without looking at the answers. If the child's answers are still incorrect, work through these questions together. Demonstrate the correct technique if necessary.

- If the child struggles with particular question types or areas, help him or her to develop the skills and strategies needed.

Answers

Section 1 Test 1 (pages 4–5)

1. B

2. C

3. A

4. D

5. building sandcastles and swimming in the sea

6. difficult, exciting

   Award 1 mark for each correctly ticked word. If more than two words are ticked, deduct 1 mark for every extra word ticked.

7. Tom's snoring kept Jake awake.

   Award 2 marks for a correct answer.

8. Jake's nose got sunburnt. or Jake's nose went bright red.

   Award 2 marks for a correct answer.

9. Jake was happy to be home because the weather was cooler and he could sleep in his own bedroom.

   Award 2 marks for answers referring to the cooler weather and 2 marks for answers stating that he could sleep in his own bedroom.

10. a) build
    b) creative
    c) wings
    d) nostrils
    e) sculptures
    f) tide

Section 1 Test 2 (pages 6–7)

1. a) walked
   b) sings
   c) ate
   d) was

   This question is testing the child's understanding of verb tense and verb–subject agreement. Children could use time adverbs (such as 'today' and 'yesterday') as clues to what tense they need to use.

2. a) and
   b) but
   c) and
   d) but

   This question is testing the child's understanding of how co-ordinating conjunctions ('and' and 'but') link ideas in a sentence in different ways ('and' links two things or ideas, whereas 'but' introduces a contrast).

3. a) very, was
   b) holiday, am
   c) dinner, pizza
   d) party, birthday

   This question is testing the child's knowledge of correct word order. Both correct words must be underlined in order for the mark to be awarded.

4. a) **W**here are you going**?**
   b) **S**top right there**!**
   c) **W**hich colour do you like best**?**
   d) **G**iraffes are my favourite animals**.**

   This question is testing the child's ability to use capital letters at the start of sentences and to recognise when to use exclamation marks, question marks and full stops. Award half a mark for each capital letter and half a mark for each full stop, exclamation mark or question mark correctly inserted. In part **b**, a full stop instead of an exclamation mark at the end of the sentence is also acceptable.

5. a) digging

b) picks

c) watches

d) puts

e) collected

f) let

This question is testing the child's ability to make sense of a passage that is missing key words. To identify the correct words, they must pay attention to the meaning, verb ending and tense.

Section 1 Test 3 (pages 8–9)

1. she will → she'll

they are → they're

what is → what's

we have → we've

This question is testing the child's ability to correctly identify and decode contractions.

2. a) punishment

b) brightness

c) happiness

d) amazement

This question is testing the child's ability to use a suffix to change a verb or adjective into a noun. If necessary, draw the child's attention to the spelling change (from 'y' to 'i') needed in part **c**.

3. a) pour

b) seem

c) flour

d) whole

This question is testing the child's ability to distinguish between common homophones.

4. a) There are 30 child**ren** in my class.

b) Sophie bought some new clot**he**s in the sale.

c) I think my mother is really be**au**tiful.

d) Malek fell beh**in**d with his piano practice.

This question is testing the child's ability to spell common exception words.

5. a) heavy

b) slow

c) strong

d) meet

e) hard

f) far

This question is testing the child's knowledge of antonyms (opposites).

Answers

Section 1 Test 4 (pages 10–11)

1. B

2. B

3. C

4. A

5. The first little chicken wishes for a worm.

   Award 2 marks for a correct answer.

6. The second little chicken shrugs.

   Award 2 marks for a correct answer.

7. yellow, green

   Award 1 mark for each correctly ticked word. If more than two words are ticked, deduct 1 mark for every extra word ticked.

8. The fourth little chicken wants to find a leaf.

   Award 2 marks for a correct answer.

9. a) The mother says the chickens should come and scratch.

   Award 2 marks for a correct answer.

   b) brisk, caring

   Award 1 mark for each correctly ticked word. If more than two words are ticked, deduct 1 mark for every extra word ticked.

10. grief — worm

    patch — stone

    moan — leaf

    squeal — bug

    shrug — meal

    squirm — scratch

Section 1 Test 5 (pages 12–13)

1. a) slowly

   b) kindly

   c) happily

   d) angrily

   This question is testing the child's ability to change adjectives to adverbs. In parts **c** and **d**, the child needs to remember to change the 'y' to an 'i'.

2. a) because

   b) if

   c) because

   d) if

   This question is testing the child's understanding of how subordinating conjunctions ('if' and 'because') link ideas in a sentence in different ways.

3. a) How old are you**?**

   b) That's not fair**!**

   c) I hate cheese**!**

   d) My name is Sara**.**

   This question is testing the child's ability to use exclamation marks, question marks and full stops. In parts **b** and **c**, a full stop instead of an exclamation mark at the end of the sentence is also acceptable.

4. a) Jamie swam fast.

   b) My mum drank a cup of tea.

   c) Elodie climbed the tree.

   d) I leapt/leaped over the fence.

   This question is testing the child's understanding of verb tense and verb–subject agreement. In part **d**, either 'leapt' or 'leaped' is acceptable.

5. a) pet

   b) lazy

   c) paws

   d) tip

   e) lap

   f) purr

   This question is testing the child's ability to make sense of a passage that is missing key words. To identify the correct words, they must pay attention to the meaning of the passage.

Schofield & Sims

Section 1 Test 6 (pages 14–15)

1. **a)** I like to padd**le** in the paddling pool.
   b) It was a truly magic**al** show.
   c) There are 20 peop**le** on the bus.
   d) Sheena won a speci**al** award for her hard work.

   This question is testing the child's ability to spell words ending in **–al** or **–le**.

2. **a)** bank circle drive fair
   b) lion mice olive tiger
   c) trick under vine wand
   d) plant quick right sheep

   This question is testing the child's knowledge of alphabetical order.

3. **a)** see
   b) course
   c) write
   d) route

   This question is testing the child's ability to distinguish between common homophones.

4. **a)** wireless
   b) hateful
   c) boastful
   d) homeless

   This question is testing the child's ability to add the suffix **–ful** or **–less** to a word to change it into an adjective.

5. **a)** middle
   b) crush
   c) clever
   d) stop
   e) break
   f) giggle

   This question is testing the child's ability to identify synonyms.

Section 2 Test 1 (pages 16–17)

1. C

2. B

3. C

4. D

5. bracelet or necklace or crown
   Award 1 mark for each correct answer. (Maximum 2 marks.)

6. You should thread it through the slit of the first daisy.
   Award 2 marks for a correct answer.

7. It means to keep on doing it again and again.
   Award 2 marks for a correct answer.

8. decorations or art projects or (birthday) cards
   Award 1 mark for each correct answer. (Maximum 2 marks.)

9. Making daisy chains would be best if you had one afternoon, because they are quick and easy to make or because the pressed flowers take weeks.
   Award 2 marks for choosing the daisy chain activity, and 2 marks for stating either that the daisy chain activity is quick or that the flower-pressing activity takes a long time.

10. **a)** belong
    b) except
    c) types
    d) petals
    e) find
    f) garden

Answers

Section 2 Test 2 (pages 18–19)

1. a) am singing
   b) is eating
   c) are telling
   d) are riding

   This question is testing the child's understanding of verb tense and verb–subject agreement.

2. a) **O**ur dog **S**pot has a long tail.
   b) **D**o **I** look older than you?
   c) **H**er sister is called **M**illy.
   d) **T**he flowers look very pretty.
   e) **W**e went to the cinema on **S**aturday.
   f) **S**he asked me if **I** liked her.

   This question is testing the child's understanding of how to use capital letters at the start of sentences, for names, for the days of the week and for the pronoun 'I'. Award 1 mark for each correctly punctuated sentence.

3. a) caravan
   b) music
   c) dinner
   d) presents

   This question is testing the child's ability to identify nouns. If the child struggles, remind them that nouns are words that name things.

4. a) is, old
   b) Jackson, name
   c) school, walk
   d) chocolate, I

   This question is testing the child's knowledge of correct word order. Both correct words must be underlined in order for the mark to be awarded.

5. a) ran
   b) gives
   c) went
   d) did

   This question is testing the child's understanding of verb tense and verb–subject agreement. Children could use time adverbs (such as 'yesterday') as clues to what tense they need to use.

Section 2 Test 3 (pages 20–21)

1. a) turkeys
   b) factories
   c) goats
   d) trolleys

   This question is testing the children's understanding of regular plurals (part **c**) and plurals of words ending in 'y' (parts **a**, **b** and **d**).

2. a) sleep (all the other words are movement verbs)
   b) sob (all the other words are actions showing happiness)
   c) cold (all the other words are synonyms for 'hot')
   d) whale (all the other words are colours)

   This question is testing the child's vocabulary and their ability to identify similarities and differences in word meaning in order to find the odd one out.

3. a) sunny
   b) always
   c) skipping
   d) stopping

   This question is testing the child's ability to spell words with or without double consonants.

4. a) along   chair   lift   tree
   b) roof   stair   wind   yellow
   c) drift   enjoy   milk   party
   d) hound   oven   silk   trail

   This question is testing the child's knowledge of alphabetical order.

5. a) sure
   b) buy
   c) deer
   d) blew
   e) won
   f) too

   This question is testing the child's ability to distinguish between common homophones.

Section 2 Test 4 (pages 22–23)

1. C

2. B

3. C

4. A

5. Penny's mum says Penny's gran should be keeping an eye on her.

   Award 2 marks for a correct answer.

6. Dr. Cement is Penny's mum's boss.

   Award 2 marks for a correct answer.

7. Everyone calls Dr. Cement 'Dr. Bugeye' because he has bulgy eyes or because he has eyes like hard-boiled eggs.

   Award 2 marks for giving one of the reasons above.

8. Penny lives on Rollins Road.

   Award 2 marks for a correct answer.

9. No, Penny doesn't think she is to blame because she says that it is not her fault or because she says that she is a victim.

   Award 2 marks for a negative answer, and 2 marks for giving one of the reasons above.

10. a) ha**pp**ens
    b) wait**in**g
    c) fr**ie**nd
    d) w**ee**k
    e) bec**au**se
    f) st**un**g

Section 2 Test 5 (pages 24–25)

1. a) **W**hat time is it**?**
   b) **I** am going swimming this afternoon**.**
   c) **W**atch out**!**
   d) **S**he has a pet mouse**.**
   e) **Y**ou are so funny**!**
   f) **D**o you like cake**?**

   This question is testing the child's understanding of how to use capital letters at the start of a sentence and when to use full stops, question marks or exclamation marks at the end of a sentence. Award half a mark for each capital letter at the beginning of the sentence and half a mark for each correct full stop, exclamation mark or question mark. (Maximum 6 marks.) In part **e**, a full stop instead of an exclamation mark at the end of the sentence is also acceptable.

2. a) waved
   b) filled
   c) threw
   d) dive

   This question is testing the child's ability to identify verbs. If the child struggles, ask them to look for the 'doing word' or action in each sentence.

3. a) My dog**'**s collar is green.
   b) The lady**'**s car was very fast.
   c) Charlie**'**s dinner was very tasty.
   d) The shop**'**s door was locked.

   This question is testing the child's ability to use apostrophes to show singular possession.

4. a) and
   b) or
   c) when
   d) because

   This question is testing the child's understanding of how subordinating ('when' and 'because') and co-ordinating ('and' and 'or') conjunctions link ideas in a sentence in different ways.

5. a) sadly
   b) merrily
   c) hungrily
   d) possibly

   This question is testing the child's ability to change adjectives into adverbs. If necessary, draw the child's attention to the spelling changes in parts **b** and **c** (from 'y' to 'i') and part **d** (the 'y' replaces the 'e').

Section 2 Test 6 (pages 26–27)

1. **a)** The clown jug**gl**ed five oranges.

b) She was su**rp**rised at the cost of the meal.

c) The traveller was expl**or**ing the forest.

d) The racing dri**ve**r was very fast.

2. **a)** messy

b) open

c) decrease

d) frowning

e) different

f) destroy

This question is testing the child's knowledge of antonyms (opposites).

3. **a)** hairbrush

b) upset

c) cannot

d) seaside

This question is testing the child's knowledge of compound words.

4. **a)** children

b) boxes

c) fences

d) mice

This question is testing the child's understanding of regular (parts **b** and **c**) and irregular (parts **a** and **d**) plurals.

5. **a)** didn't

b) aren't

c) shouldn't

d) isn't

This question is testing the child's ability to correctly add an apostrophe to a contraction. You could point out that in this question, the apostrophe is replacing the letter 'o' in 'not' rather than marking the space between the two words – so 'didn't' rather than 'did'nt'.

Section 3 Test 1 (pages 28–29)

1. D

2. B

3. D

4. C

5. There are five verses in the poem.

Award 2 marks for a correct answer.

6. The wind is 'flying from somewhere as fast as it can'.

Award 2 marks for a correct answer.

7. He could let go of his kite and the wind would blow it away. Then he would look for his kite and the place where he found it would be where the wind had gone.

Award 2 marks for answers stating that he would let go of the kite and it would blow away, and 2 marks for mentioning that where he found his kite would be where the wind had gone.

8. No, the writer never figures out where the wind comes from.

Award 2 marks for a negative answer.

9. **a)** goes   **b)** night

10. **a)** air

b) mountains

c) lakes

d) heat

e) cool

f) rushes

Answers

Section 3 Test 2 (pages 30–31)

1. **a)** faster
   b) tiniest
   c) louder
   d) wisest

   In this question, the child has to decide whether to write a comparative or superlative adjective. The use of 'the' directly before the adjective is an indication that a superlative is required.
   In part **b**, the child might also forget to change the spelling from 'tiny' to 'tiniest'.

2. **a)** Zac's book was very exciting.
   b) Suki's teapot was made of china.
   c) The cat's milk was in her bowl.
   d) The man's voice was very loud.

   This question is testing the child's ability to use apostrophes to show singular possession.

3. **a)** there, aunt
   b) cold, is
   c) tweeted, bird
   d) fiercely, The
   e) brightly, sun
   f) hot, was

   This question is testing the child's knowledge of correct word order. Both correct words must be underlined in order for the mark to be awarded.

4. **a)** was dancing
   b) were swinging
   c) was shouting
   d) were hiding

   This question is testing the child's understanding of verb tense and verb–subject agreement.

5. **a)** My sister put on her coat, hat, gloves and scarf.
   b) We have three pet cats, two dogs, a hamster and a rabbit.
   c) His jumper was red, green, yellow and orange.
   d) I had a large dinner of fish, chips, beans and peas.

   This question is testing the child's ability to use commas in lists. Award half a mark for each correctly inserted comma. (Maximum 4 marks.)

Answers

Section 3 Test 3 (pages 32–33)

1. **a)** cuddled

    b) brave

    c) clean

    d) miserably

    e) chat

    f) contest

    This question is testing the child's ability to identify synonyms.

2. **a)** Jack's dad b**ak**ed him a birthday cake.

    b) My brother loves b**ou**ncing on the trampoline.

    c) You must be c**ar**eful not to cut yourself.

    d) The broken watch was usel**es**s.

    This question is testing the child's ability to spell words that contain suffixes.

3. **a)** rainbow

    b) bookshelf

    c) cupcake

    d) into

    This question is testing the child's knowledge of compound words.

4. **a)** drop (all the other words are synonyms for 'hold')

    b) sit (all the other words are movement verbs)

    c) jewel (all the other words are types of metal)

    d) swan (all the other words end in 'key')

    This question is testing the child's vocabulary and their ability to identify common features of words in order to find the odd one out.

5. **a)** wrist

    b) knife

    c) gnomes

    d) knees

    This question is testing the child's ability to spell words starting with silent letters.

Section 3 Test 4 (pages 34–35)

1. C

2. B

3. A

4. C

5. The little sister was given a basket so she could put stones in it or because she liked to collect stones.

    Award 2 marks for either of the reasons given above.

6. Their mother said that the little sister should not go near the water or the little sister should not get herself wet.

    Award 2 marks for either of the reasons given above.

7. socks, shoes

    Award 1 mark for each correctly ticked answer. If more than two words are ticked, deduct 1 mark for every extra word ticked.

8. fishing-nets, jam-jars

    Award 1 mark for each correctly ticked answer. If more than two words are ticked, deduct 1 mark for every extra word ticked.

9. The children filled their jam-jars with water so they could put fish in them.

    Award 2 marks for a correct answer.

10. No, the children did not catch any fish.

    Award 2 marks for a negative answer.

11. The little sister went into the water. or The little sister went fishing. or The little sister got wet.

    Award 2 marks for any of the answers given above.

12. Answers will vary according to the child. Example answers: Yes, I do think she was naughty because she went into the water even though she had been told not to. or No, I don't think she was naughty because she just wanted to join in the fun.

    Award 2 marks for giving an opinion and 2 marks for giving a suitable reason.

Section 3 Test 5 (pages 36–37)

1. **a)** I won the painting competition.

   b) There are seven colours in the rainbow.

   c) I have a cat called Mittens.

   d) My brother is a vegetarian.

   This question is testing the child's knowledge of correct word order.

2. **I** have three pet rabbits called **F**lossy**, F**luffy and **F**izz**. T**hey live in a big hutch in my garden**. F**lossy and **F**luffy are white and **F**izz is grey**.**

   This question is testing the child's ability to use capital letters at the start of sentences and for names, and to recognise when to use full stops and commas. There are 12 errors in total. Award half a mark for each correctly inserted capital letter or punctuation mark. (Maximum 6 marks.)

3. **a)** went

   b) makes

   c) walking

   d) doesn't

   This question is testing the child's understanding of verb tense and verb–subject agreement. Children could use time adverbs (such as 'tomorrow') as clues to what tense they need to use.

4. **a)** if

   b) that

   c) or

   d) but

   This question is testing the child's understanding of how subordinating ('if' and 'that') and co-ordinating ('or' and 'but') conjunctions link ideas in a sentence in different ways.

5. **a)** silver

   b) shiny

   c) funny

   d) fluffy

   This question is testing the child's ability to identify adjectives. In parts **c** and **d**, they must distinguish between adjectives and adverbs ('really' and 'very'). You could point out that the adjective usually comes directly before the noun.

Section 3 Test 6 (pages 38–39)

1. **a)** fable, story

   b) simple, easy

   c) special, unusual

   d) lady, woman

   This question is testing the child's ability to identify synonyms.

2. **a)** airport

   b) firework

   c) without

   d) nowhere

   This question is testing the child's knowledge of compound words.

3. **a)** person

   b) finish

   c) packet

   d) window

   This question is testing the child's understanding of what a syllable is and ability to spell two-syllable words.

4. **a)** stop, start

   b) quiet, noisy

   c) push, pull

   d) under, over

   e) inside, outside

   f) give, take

   This question is testing the child's knowledge of antonyms (opposites).

5. **a)** easy   home   loud   slow

   b) drip   dust   seek   sing

   c) hand   kind   lazy   live

   d) warm   week   wish   work

   This question is testing the child's knowledge of alphabetical order.

This book of answers is a pull-out section from **English Rapid Tests 1**.

Published by **Schofield & Sims Ltd**,
7 Mariner Court, Wakefield, West Yorkshire WF4 3FL, UK
Telephone 01484 607080
www.schofieldandsims.co.uk

This edition copyright © Schofield & Sims Ltd, 2018
First published in 2018

Author: **Siân Goodspeed**. Siân Goodspeed has asserted her moral rights under the
Copyright, Designs and Patents Act, 1988, to be identified as the author of this work.

British Library Cataloguing in Publication Data. A catalogue record for this book
is available from the British Library.

Design by **Ledgard Jepson Ltd**
Printed in the UK by **Page Bros (Norwich) Ltd**

ISBN 978 07217 1429 5

Schofield & Sims

4. Write out the words in each row on the line so that they are in alphabetical order.

Example: hope   brick   wand   swap   <u>brick   hope   swap   wand</u>

a) tree   along   chair   lift

_____

b) wind   yellow   stair   roof

_____

c) milk   drift   enjoy   party

_____

d) silk   hound   trail   oven

_____

/4

5. Decide which of the words in bold is the correct word for each sentence. Underline the word.

Example: Maddy was wearing a **<u>plain</u> / plane** scarf.

a) Are you **shore / sure** you don't want any tea?

b) My parents are going to **buy / by** me a new school bag.

c) The **deer / dear** leapt across the field.

d) The wind **blew / blue** the fence over.

e) I was proud when I **won / one** the race.

f) Kadri would like a jam sandwich **to / too**.

/6

Score:		Time taken:		Target met?	

Target time: **12 minutes**

Read the text and answer the questions below.

Extract from **Penny Dreadful is Incredibly Contagious, by Joanna Nadin**

My name is not actually Penny Dreadful. It is Penelope Jones. The "Dreadful" bit is my dad's JOKE. I know it is a joke because every time he says it he laughs like a honking goose. But I do not see the funny side.

5   Plus it is not even true that I am dreadful. It is, like Gran says, i.e. that I am a MAGNET FOR DISASTER. Mum says if Gran kept a better eye on me in the first place instead of on *Rumbaba* in the two o'clock at Epsom then I might not be quite so magnetic.

But Gran says if Mum wasn't so busy answering phones for Dr. Cement, who is her boss, and who has bulgy eyes like hard-boiled eggs (which is why everyone calls him Dr. Bugeye), and Dad wasn't so
10 busy solving crises at the council, then they would be able to solve some crises at 73 Rollins Road, i.e. our house. So you see it is completely not my fault.

For instance, it is not my fault that Bridget Grimes is in BIG TROUBLE for toppling the model of the
15 Leaning Tower of Pisa made entirely out of playing cards. It is because we are VICTIMS OF CIRCUMSTANCE (which means everything else that is happening in the world around you) and the CIRCUMSTANCES are:

20 a) A wasp
    2. A factory that makes fish fingers
    c) Miss Patterson's GOLDEN OPPORTUNITY

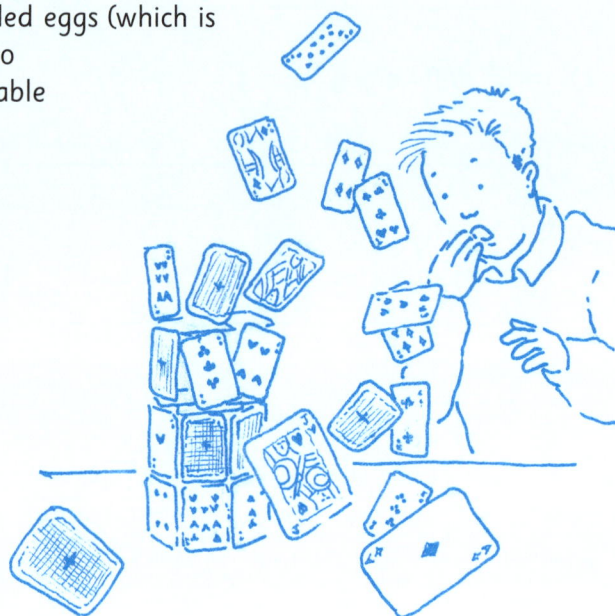

Write **A**, **B**, **C** or **D** on the answer line.

1. What is Penny's surname?

  A Dreadful

  B Smith

  C Jones

  D Cement

_____   /1

2. What does Penny say her dad sounds like when he laughs?

  A a donkey

  B a goose

  C a camel

  D a cow

_____   /1

3. What does Penny think of her nickname?

  A She thinks it is funny.

  B She is proud of it.

  C She does not think it is fair.

  D She thinks it suits her.

_____   /1

4. Why does Gran say Penny is a 'magnet for disaster'?

  A Penny always gets into trouble.

  B Penny tells lots of jokes.

  C Penny is very lucky.

  D Penny is always busy.

_____   /1

5. Who does Penny's mum say is meant to be keeping an eye on her?

_____

_____ /2

6. Who is Dr. Cement?

_____

_____ /2

7. Why does everyone call Dr. Cement 'Dr. Bugeye'?

_____

_____ /2

8. What street does Penny live on?

_____

_____ /2

9. Does Penny think she is to blame for any of the 'disasters' that happen when she is around? Explain your answer.

_____

_____

_____

_____ /4

10. Here is the next part of the story. The words in bold have some letters missing. Fill in the letters of these incomplete words so that the passage makes sense.

What **a) ha___ ___ens** is that I am on the corner of Newton Street trying to persuade

a worm to climb on a pigeon feather (only the worm is not KEEN on the feather, he would

rather climb on some mud), and also **b) wait___ ___g** for Cosmo Moon Webster (who is

my best **c) fr___ ___nd** even though he is a **d) w___ ___k** older and a boy) when his mum

(who is called Sunflower even though her real name is Barbara) comes out of the house

completely quickly and ALL OF A FLUSTER. She says there has been an ACCIDENT and

also an INJURY **e) bec___ ___se** Cosmo has been **f) st___ ___g** on the ear by a WASP. /6

| Score: | | Time taken: | | Target met? | |

Target time: **12 minutes**

1. The sentences below are missing their punctuation. Write out each sentence on the line, adding in the correct sentence punctuation.

Example: my brother likes cheese   My brother likes cheese.

a) what time is it

_____

b) i am going swimming this afternoon

_____

c) watch out

_____

d) she has a pet mouse

_____

e) you are so funny

_____

f) do you like cake

_____

/6

2. Underline the verb in each sentence.

Example: I <u>jumped</u> over the hedge.

a) We waved at our friends.

b) Dad filled the bath with warm water.

c) I threw the ball a long way.

d) You dive very gracefully.

/4

3. Add in the missing apostrophes to the sentences below.

Example: My sister's dress is blue.

a) My dogs collar is green.

b) The ladys car was very fast.

c) Charlies dinner was very tasty.

d) The shops door was locked.

/4

4. Choose the best word, **when**, **or**, **and** or **because**, to complete each sentence. Write it on the line. You should use each word only once.

Example: I wore my coat _because_ it was cold.

a) Anika put on her shoes _____ tied up her laces.

b) Would you like jam _____ honey on your toast?

c) You should get out of bed _____ your alarm goes off.

d) I had to redo my homework _____ I lost it.

/4

5. Change each word in bold into an adverb so that the sentence makes sense. Write the adverb on the line.

Example: Emma ran **quick** down the road.   _quickly_

a) Leo looked **sad** at the mess.   _____

b) She rowed **merry** down the river.   _____

c) Ollie looked at the food **hungry**.   _____

d) You can't **possible** jump from that height!   _____

/4

Score:	Time taken:	Target met?

Target time: **12 minutes**

1. Each sentence below contains an incomplete word. Write out the sentence on the line, filling in the missing letters to spell the word correctly.

Example: I **wo** ___ ___**d** like to see the ballet.   _I would like to see the ballet._

a) The clown **jug** ___ ___**ed** five oranges.

_____

b) She was **su** ___ ___**rised** at the cost of the meal.

_____

c) The traveller was **expl** ___ ___**ing** the forest.

_____

d) The racing **dri** ___ ___**r** was very fast.

_____

/4

2. Underline the word in each set of brackets that means the <u>opposite</u> of the word in bold.

Example: up   (left   yes   <u>down</u>)

a) tidy   (clean   room   messy)

b) close   (open   near   door)

c) increase   (double   decrease   add)

d) smiling   (frowning   laughing   cry)

e) same   (odd   like   different)

f) build   (tower   destroy   make)

/6

3. One word from the first set of brackets goes together with one word from the second set of brackets to make a new word. Underline the two words and write the new word on the line.

Example: (<u>out</u> not but)　　(or <u>side</u> dip)　　　　_outside_

a) (look hair swing)　　(brush jump play)　　　_____

b) (up red night)　　　　(it set down)　　　　　_____

c) (war win can)　　　　(sing not pot)　　　　_____

d) (see saw sea)　　　　(sun jar side)　　　　_____

/4

4. Write the plural form of each word on the line.

Example: house　　_houses_

a) child　　　　_____

b) box　　　　_____

c) fence　　　_____

d) mouse　　　_____

/4

5. Add an apostrophe in the correct place in each contraction.

Example: cannot　⟶　c a n't

a) did not　　⟶　d i d n t

b) are not　　⟶　a r e n t

c) should not　⟶　s h o u l d n t

d) is not　　⟶　i s n t

/4

Score:		Time taken:		Target met?	

Target time: **12 minutes**

Read the text and answer the questions below.

Wind on the Hill, by A. A. Milne

No one can tell me,
Nobody knows,
Where the wind comes from,
Where the wind goes.

5 It's flying from somewhere
As fast as it can,
I couldn't keep up with it,
Not if I ran.

But if I stopped holding
10 The string of my kite,
It would blow with the wind
For a day and a night.

And then when I found it,
Wherever it blew,
15 I should know that the wind
Had been going there too.

So then I could tell them
Where the wind goes...
But where the wind comes from
20 Nobody knows.

Write **A**, **B**, **C** or **D** on the answer line.

1. What is this poem about?

A the changing seasons

B a stormy day

C somebody who lost their kite

D somebody wondering where the wind comes from

_____ /1

2. In the poem, what does nobody know?

A how to fly a kite

B where the wind comes from

C if it is night-time

D how windy it is

_____ /1

3. Which of the following is most likely to be the setting for this poem?

A a hot summer's day

B a sunny spring day

C a cold, still winter's day

D a blustery autumn day

_____ /1

4. What is the author holding on to?

A a ball

B a net

C a kite

D a hat

_____ /1

5. How many verses does this poem have?

_____ /2

6. What is 'flying from somewhere as fast as it can'?

_____ /2

7. What does the author say he could do to find out where the wind goes to?

_____

_____

_____

_____ /4

8. Does the author figure out where the wind comes from?

_____ /2

9. Find a word in the poem that rhymes with each word below.

a) knows _____   **b)** kite _____ /2

10. The passage below has had some words removed. Choose the correct words from the box. Write the missing words on the lines. You may use each word only once.

air   mountains   rushes   heat   lakes   cool

Wind is moving air. The **a)** _____ moves when heat from the Sun

warms the Earth. The Earth's surface is made up of areas of land (such as forests,

b) _____ and deserts) and areas of water (such as oceans, rivers and

c) _____). In the daytime, the Sun warms all of these different areas,

but the air above land takes in the Sun's **d)** _____ faster than the air

above water. Warm air is lighter than **e)** _____ air, so the warm air over

the land rises and the cooler air over the water **f)** _____ in to take the

place of the warmer air. This movement of air is what makes the wind blow. /6

Score:		Time taken:		Target met?	

Target time: **12 minutes**

1. Change each adjective in bold so that the sentence makes sense. Write the new word on the line.

Example: My brother is **old** than me. _older_

a) Lucia was **fast** than Petra. _____

b) She was the **tiny** baby Dan had ever seen. _____

c) The robin chirped much **loud** than the sparrow. _____

d) The owl is the **wise** of birds. _____

/4

2. Add in the missing apostrophes to the sentences below.

Example: My sister's dress is blue.

a) Zacs book was very exciting.

b) Sukis teapot was made of china.

c) The cats milk was in her bowl.

d) The mans voice was very loud.

/4

3. In each of the sentences below, <u>two</u> of the words have swapped places. Work out which words need to be swapped for the sentence to make sense. Underline the two words.

Example: My <u>likes</u> <u>sister</u> playing football.

a) My there lives aunt.

b) It cold is today.

c) The tweeted bird loudly.

d) fiercely dog barked The.

e) The brightly is shining sun.

f) He hot very was and thirsty.

/6

4. Read the sentences below and look at the words in bold. Change the present tense into the past tense by changing the words in bold. Write the new words on the line.

The first one has been done for you.

Present tense	Past tense
Example: I **am jumping** on my trampoline.	*was jumping*
a) He **is dancing** on the rooftops.	_____
b) They **are swinging** from the monkey bars.	_____
c) Freya **is shouting** very loudly.	_____
d) You **are hiding** from your friend.	_____

/4

5. The sentences below are missing their commas. Write out each sentence on the line, adding in the correct comma or commas.

a) My sister put on her coat hat gloves and scarf.

_____

b) We have three pet cats two dogs a hamster and a rabbit.

_____

c) His jumper was red green yellow and orange.

_____

d) I had a large dinner of fish chips beans and peas.

_____

/4

Score:		Time taken:		Target met?	

Target time: **12 minutes**

1. Underline the word in each set of brackets that is <u>closest</u> in meaning to the word in bold.

Example: big   (small   run   <u>large</u>)

a) **hugged**   (holds   large   cuddled)

b) **fearless**   (scared   brave   lost)

c) **wash**   (wet   clean   dry)

d) **sadly**   (angrily   miserably   happily)

e) **conversation**   (argue   save   chat)

f) **competition**   (contest   winner   loser)

/6

2. Each sentence below contains an incomplete word. Write out the sentence on the line, filling in the missing letters to spell the word correctly.

**Example: I wo___ ___d like to see the ballet.   <u>I would like to see the ballet.</u>

a) Jack's dad **b___ ___ed** him a birthday cake.

_____

b) My brother loves **b___ ___ncing** on the trampoline.

_____

c) You must be **c___ ___eful** not to cut yourself.

_____

d) The broken watch was **usel___ ___s.**

_____

/4

3. One word from the first set of brackets goes together with one word from the second set of brackets to make a new word. Underline the two words and write the new word on the line.

Example: (<u>out</u> not but)   (or <u>side</u> dip)   <u>outside</u>

a) (cloud rain sun)   (bow moon snow)   _____

b) (tale story book)   (page shelf dream)   _____

c) (glass cup mug)   (eat drink cake)   _____

d) (in up out)   (to down round)   _____

/4

4. One word in each set does not go with the others. Underline this odd word out.

Example: paint draw scribble <u>dance</u>

a) grab hold drop grasp

b) sit walk jump skip

c) silver gold jewel bronze

d) donkey monkey swan turkey

/4

5. In each sentence below, there is an incorrectly spelt word. Find the word, underline it and then write the correct spelling on the line.

Example: She found the test <u>dificult</u>.   <u>difficult</u>

a) My sister fell over and broke her rist.   _____

b) Sue cut the cheese with a sharp nife.   _____

c) We have lots of nomes in our garden.   _____

d) I have patches on the nees of my trousers.   _____

/4

Score:		Time taken:		Target met?	

Target time: **12 minutes**

Read the text and answer the questions below.

Extract from **My Naughty Little Sister Goes Fishing, by Dorothy Edwards**

One day, when I was a little girl, and my sister was a very little girl, some children came to our house and asked my mother if I could go fishing with them. They had jam-jars with string on them, and fishing-nets and sandwiches and lemonade. My mother said, "Yes" – I could go with them; and she found *me* a jam-jar and a fishing-net, and cut *me* some sandwiches.

5   Then my naughty little sister said, "I want to go! I want to go!" Just like that. So my mother said I might as well take her too.

Then my mother cut some sandwiches for my little sister, but she didn't give her a jam-jar or a fishing-net because she said she was too little to go near the water. My mother gave my little sister a basket to put stones in, because my little sister liked to pick up stones, and she gave me a big bottle of lemonade
10 to carry for both of us.

My mother said, "You mustn't let your little sister get herself wet. You must keep her away from the water."

And I said, "All right, Mother, I promise."

So then we went off to the little river, and we took our shoes off and our socks off, and tucked up our clothes, and we went into the water to catch
15 fish with our fishing-nets, and we filled our jam-jars with water to put the fishes in when we caught them. And we said to my naughty little sister, "You mustn't come, you'll get yourself wet."

Well, we paddled and paddled and fished and fished, but we didn't catch any fish at all, not one little tiny one even. Then a boy said,
20 "Look, there is your little sister in the water too!"

And, do you know, my naughty little sister had walked right into the water with her shoes and socks on, and she was trying to fish with her little basket.

Write **A**, **B**, **C** or **D** on the answer line.

1. Where were the children going?
    A to the park
    B to the shops
    C to a river
    D to school

    _____   /1

2. What activity were the children going to do?
    A swimming
    B fishing
    C painting
    D hiking

    _____   /1

3. What did the children take to eat?
    A sandwiches
    B biscuits
    C cakes
    D crisps

    _____   /1

4. What did the children take to drink?
    A orange juice
    B water
    C lemonade
    D blackcurrant squash

    _____   /1

5. Why was the little sister given a basket to take with her?

_____

_____ /2

6. What warning did the mother give about the little sister before they left the house?

_____

_____ /2

7. Which <u>two</u> items of clothing did the children remove before fishing? Tick the boxes.

hats ☐   socks ☐   coats ☐   shoes ☐   shorts ☐   /2

8. Which <u>two</u> things did the children use for fishing? Tick the boxes.

fishing rods ☐   buckets ☐   fishing-nets ☐   spades ☐   jam-jars ☐   /2

9. Why did the children fill their jam-jars with water?

_____

_____ /2

10. Did the children catch any fish?

_____ /2

11. What did the little sister do that she wasn't allowed to do?

_____

_____ /2

12. Do you think the author's little sister was naughty? Explain your answer.

_____

_____

_____

_____ /4

Score: _____   Time taken: _____   Target met? _____

Target time: **12 minutes**

1. Unjumble each sentence so that it makes sense. Write out the correct sentence on the line.

   Example: My likes sister football playing.   My sister likes playing football.

   a) painting I the won competition.

   _____

   b) rainbow There colours the are seven in.

   _____

   c) have Mittens called a cat I.

   _____

   d) vegetarian My is a brother.

   _____

   /4

2. The passage below contains no punctuation. Write out the passage on the lines, adding in the correct punctuation. Look out for capital letters, full stops, exclamation marks, question marks and commas.

   i have three pet rabbits called flossy fluffy and fizz they live in a big hutch in my garden flossy and fluffy are white and fizz is grey

   _____

   _____

   _____

   _____

   /6

3. Read the sentences below. Underline the correct verb form in each set of brackets.

Example: I always (<u>jump</u> jumped jumping) high on my trampoline.

a) Last week, Tyler (gone went go) to a birthday party.

b) On school days, my dad (make makes making) me a packed lunch.

c) Tomorrow, we are (walks walked walking) to school.

d) Ava (don't doesn't do) like the colour pink.

/4

4. Choose the best word, **but**, **or**, **that** or **if**, to complete each sentence. Write it on the line. You may use each word only once.

Example: I like coffee <u> but </u> I don't like tea.

a) I will be sad _____ you ruin my picture.

b) She told me _____ she was eight years old.

c) Would you like popcorn _____ a bag of sweets?

d) He is tall _____ his friend is even taller.

/4

5. Underline the adjective in each sentence.

Example: The <u>large</u> cat sat on the wall.

a) Isabelle's father has a silver car.

b) My coat has many shiny buttons.

c) Arjun told me a really funny joke.

d) I have a pair of very fluffy slippers.

/4

Score:	Time taken:	Target met?

Target time: **12 minutes**

1. Underline the two words (one in each set of brackets) that are <u>closest</u> in meaning.

    Example: (small run <u>large</u>)   (up walk <u>big</u>)

    a) (kettle fable bottle)   (story tell mug)

    b) (simple hard strong)   (soft easy light)

    c) (kind special magic)   (unusual wand cross)

    d) (lady man uncle)   (aunt woman boy)

/4

2. One word from the first set of brackets goes together with one word from the second set of brackets to make a new word. Underline the two words and write the new word on the line.

    Example: (<u>out</u> not but)   (or <u>side</u> dip)   <u>outside</u>

    a) (end air cloud)   (plain sky port)   _____

    b) (fire trick bite)   (work bear food)   _____

    c) (post cap with)   (ate mail out)   _____

    d) (why yes no)   (way win where)   _____

/4

3. Add the second syllable to these words. For each one, choose an ending from the box below. Write the new word on the line.

    | son   ow   ish   et   en |

    Example: bask_____   ⟶   <u>basket</u>

    a) per_____   ⟶   _____

    b) fin_____   ⟶   _____

    c) pack_____   ⟶   _____

    d) wind_____   ⟶   _____

/4

4. Underline the two words (one in each set of brackets) that are <u>opposite</u> in meaning.

Example: (<u>small</u> out in)   (up <u>large</u> little)

a) (stand sit stop)   (start steer stink)

b) (quiet quite queen)   (nosy noisy nasty)

c) (put push pick)   (place pull pat)

d) (round next under)   (over about to)

e) (garden inside house)   (outside grass home)

f) (reach give ask)   (grant take lift)

/6

5. Write out the words in each row on the line so that they are in alphabetical order.

Example: hope brick wand swap   <u>brick   hope   swap   wand</u>

a) slow home loud easy

_____

b) drip sing dust seek

_____

c) live hand lazy kind

_____

d) work warm wish week

_____

/4

Score:		Time taken:		Target met?	

Progress chart

Write the score (out of 22) for each test in the box provided on the right of the graph.
Then colour in the row next to the box to represent this score.

Section 1

		Total
Test 1		
Test 2		
Test 3		
Test 4		
Test 5		
Test 6		

1 2 3 4 5 6 7 8 9 10 11 12 13 14 15 16 17 18 19 20 21 22

Score (out of 22)

Section 2

		Total
Test 1		
Test 2		
Test 3		
Test 4		
Test 5		
Test 6		

1 2 3 4 5 6 7 8 9 10 11 12 13 14 15 16 17 18 19 20 21 22

Score (out of 22)

Section 3

		Total
Test 1		
Test 2		
Test 3		
Test 4		
Test 5		
Test 6		

1 2 3 4 5 6 7 8 9 10 11 12 13 14 15 16 17 18 19 20 21 22

Score (out of 22)